AN IDEAS INTO ACTION GUIDEBOOK

How to Form a Team

Five Keys to High Performance

IDEAS INTO ACTION GUIDEBOOKS

Aimed at managers and executives who are concerned with their own and others' development, each guidebook in this series gives specific advice on how to complete a developmental task or solve a leadership problem.

LEAD CONTRIBUTORS	Kim Kanaga
	Michael E. Kossler
CONTRIBUTORS	Henry Browning
	Sonya Prestridge
GUIDEBOOK ADVISORY GROUP	Victoria A. Guthrie
	Cynthia D. McCauley
	Russ S. Moxley
DIRECTOR OF PUBLICATIONS	Martin Wilcox
EDITOR	Peter Scisco
WRITER	Janet Fox
DESIGN AND LAYOUT	Joanne Ferguson
CONTRIBUTING ARTISTS	Laura J. Gibson
	Chris Wilson, 29 & Company

CCL No. 414
ISBN No. 1-882197-68-2

CENTER FOR CREATIVE LEADERSHIP
POST OFFICE BOX 26300
GREENSBORO, NORTH CAROLINA 27438-6300
336-288-7210

AN IDEAS INTO ACTION GUIDEBOOK

How to Form a Team

Five Keys to High Performance

Kim Kanaga and Michael E. Kossler

Center for
Creative Leadership

leadership. learning. life.

THE IDEAS INTO ACTION GUIDEBOOK SERIES

This series of guidebooks draws on the practical knowledge that the Center for Creative Leadership (CCL) has generated in the course of more than thirty years of research and educational activity conducted in partnership with hundreds of thousands of managers and executives. Much of this knowledge is shared – in a way that is distinct from the typical university department, professional association, or consultancy. CCL is not simply a collection of individual experts, although the individual credentials of its staff are impressive; rather it is a community, with its members holding certain principles in common and working together to understand and generate practical responses to today's leadership and organizational challenges.

The purpose of the series is to provide managers with specific advice on how to complete a developmental task or solve a leadership challenge. In doing that the series carries out CCL's mission to advance the understanding, practice, and development of leadership for the benefit of society worldwide. We think you will find the Ideas Into Action Guidebooks an important addition to your leadership toolkit.

Other guidebooks currently available:
- *Ongoing Feedback: How to Get It, How to Use It*
- *Becoming a More Versatile Learner*
- *Reaching Your Development Goals*
- *Giving Feedback to Subordinates*
- *Three Keys to Development: Defining and Meeting Your Leadership Challenges*
- *Feedback That Works: How to Build and Deliver Your Message*
- *Communicating Across Cultures*
- *Learning from Life: Turning Life's Lessons into Leadership Experience*
- *Keeping Your Career on Track: Twenty Success Strategies*
- *Preparing for Development: Making the Most of Formal Leadership Programs*
- *Choosing an Executive Coach*
- *Setting Your Development Goals: Start with Your Values*
- *Do You Really Need a Team?*
- *Building Resiliency: How to Thrive in Times of Change*

Table of Contents

7   What Is a Team?

8   Forming an Effective Team
Set a Clear Direction
Build Organizational Support
Create an Empowering Team Structure
Identify Key Relationships
Monitor External Factors

27   Team Formation: A Special Event

27   Suggested Readings

28   Background

29   Key Point Summary

EXECUTIVE BRIEF

Team success doesn't start with results. It starts with the building of an effective team that can deliver on its promise. This book is for managers and leaders who have responsibility for the creation and success of teams. If you are a department head or project manager, or if you are the senior-level champion or sponsor of a proposed team, this guidebook will help you understand the five factors critical to building effective teams and show you how to use those factors to lay the groundwork for successful teams.

What Is a Team?

Many kinds of workgroups exhibit cooperative attitudes and practices and might be described as teams. But in this guidebook *team* refers to a specific kind of group whose members are collectively accountable for achieving the team's goals. Typically, a team has these five characteristics:

1. *Members of the team are dependent upon each other for the completion of a complex task.* It's often advisable to form a team when the task is complex and actually requires the interdependent efforts of a diverse group of people. This typically occurs when the members of a team represent different functional areas of an organization; for example, R&D, engineering, manufacturing, and marketing.

2. *Members possess different but complementary skill sets.* In many types of workgroups (a company's sales force, for instance), the members all possess similar perspectives and skills. A defining characteristic of a team is that members bring different sets of skills (and usually different backgrounds and perspectives) to the task. Just as an effective baseball team needs good hitters, good pitchers, and good fielders, a business team needs a combination of abilities to be effective – a combination rarely, if ever, found in a single individual.

3. *Teams manage their own work within boundaries set by the organization.* Teams are quite autonomous compared to other kinds of groups. A team may be charged with carrying out its work within a specified time period, and may be accountable to a specific individual or management group. But effective teams typically have considerable latitude in how they carry out their work. They decide for themselves how often and for how long they

7

want to meet; which members will take what kinds of responsibilities; and how they will make decisions, handle conflict, and communicate.

4. *Teams have internal processes for managing communication, resolving conflicts, solving problems, making decisions, and reaching goals.* Teams are not always bound by the same policies and practices by which the organization as a whole works. Deciding on common processes is one of the first tasks of a newly formed team.

5. *Teams are bounded and stable over time.* Some teams are formed and dissolved in a matter of a few months. Some have a life span of a few years. Others, like the management team of a company, may be a permanent fixture of the organization. In each case, stability of the membership impacts team performance.

Although teams share these five characteristics, the characteristics themselves don't guarantee that a team will be effective in meeting its goals. One of the first steps to take toward increasing team effectiveness is to pay attention to how you form your team.

Forming an Effective Team

Team effectiveness isn't inevitable. Teams quite often fail to meet performance objectives, and the consequences can be harsh and lasting. The business opportunities a team is charged with developing may be missed, the business problem a team is charged with solving may persist and even worsen, competitive advantage may be lost, relationships between business units may be damaged, trust in the organization's leadership and direction can erode, valuable people may resign, and subsequent teams may launch in an atmosphere of cynicism and doubt, increasing the likelihood that they, too, will fall short.

Yet most of the pitfalls teams encounter are predictable and preventable. In its research into teams and its work with organizational teams, CCL has learned that what a leader does or fails to do prior to and during team formation has considerable impact on the team's fate. You can head off most of the problems that beset teams by considering in advance the composition of the team, its purpose, the resources it will need, and the potential obstacles it will face.

By carefully laying the groundwork you will greatly increase the likelihood that the team you launch will deliver on its potential. You can be sure to cover all of the facets of team formation by reviewing five critical components:

1. *Set a clear direction.* A common sense of purpose unifies team members and provides a context within which they can understand how the team functions and how their own contributions play a part.

2. *Build organizational support.* Teams are more productive when they are able to operate within an organization that provides resources that support their efforts.

3. *Create a team structure that empowers team members.* Establishing shared expectations, identifying and organizing resources, and creating a clear sense of how the team goes about doing its work allows team members to focus their efforts on achieving the team's goal(s).

4. *Identify key relationships.* Building key relationships with individuals, other teams, and organizations allows more efficient and effective flow of resources into and from your team.

5. *Monitor external factors.* Gathering and analyzing information about the broader environment relevant to your team's goals enables it to make necessary adjustments when conditions warrant.

Set a Clear Direction

When teams go awry it's often the case that the team members have different ideas of what the team's mission is and what they are expected to accomplish. Effective teams begin with a clear purpose. In addition to your view of the team's purpose and direction, there are stakeholders with their own views. Talk to these stakeholders to gain an understanding of their expectations for team success. Compile this information so that you are prepared to share it with the team you're forming.

A team's purpose doesn't specify how the team will carry out its work but indicates what the end result of the team's work will be. For example, the result might be a plan for increasing sales or a strategy for penetrating a specific market. Hone your team's purpose to a strong, memorable, and inspiring challenge. Use the Team Direction Worksheet on page 11 to help you clarify your team's purpose.

Build Organizational Support

When a team fails to operate at its full potential, team members and sponsors often cite interpersonal conflicts and tensions as the reasons. But more often than not the real causes of failure lie outside the team, in the system that fielded and is meant to support the team. While forming your team make special efforts to ensure that your organization supports the team with adequate resources, organizational sponsorship, careful recognition of team member responsibility (to the team and to the organization), authority, a means of providing feedback on performance, and a team-oriented reward system.

Anticipate and obtain team resources. One measure of an organization's support for its teams is whether or not the team members have sufficient resources to accomplish their goals. Time to develop is one of the resources your team may require. It may

Team Direction Worksheet

Who made the decision to form this team?

_____

Why was that decision made?

_____

Who has a vested interest in your team's results?

_____

What are their expectations of the team?

_____

What is the nature of the work the team is expected to do?

_____

What is the team trying to accomplish?

_____

Why is this important?

_____

also need physical space, support staff, equipment, a travel budget, and training opportunities, all of which add to the bottom line. Teams are costly, and teams that fail because organizations don't give them the resources they need are extremely costly. Plan for getting your team the resources it needs using the Team Resources Worksheet on pages 16-17.

Secure sponsorship. High-level organizational sponsorship goes a long way toward setting the stage for team success. If the CEO or another top executive publicly supports your team, endorses your team's interests, and communicates your team's importance, people in your organization will perceive the team's mission as vital and urgent. That will enable your team to get the resources and system support it needs to succeed. Knowing what a potential sponsor has to gain by the team's efforts will help you solicit a sponsor or advocate for your team. For example, a vice president of sales who believes that sales force productivity and morale can be increased by adding new products would undoubtedly be a good choice to sponsor a cross-functional product development team.

Delineate responsibilities. Serving on a team often takes people away from their regular duties and can put team members in conflict with some of the interests and goals of their "home" workgroups. That tension can create divided loyalties in team members. As you form your team explain and/or negotiate with potential team members and their managers for the kind of time commitment that's required and secure their endorsement. Plan carefully – don't underestimate the amount of time a person will have to spend on the team's work.

Define authority. If your team doesn't have the authority to make decisions or to implement tactics for carrying out those decisions, its chances of success are limited. Decide what kind of authority the team will have: the power to take action, the power to make decisions, or the power to make recommendations. Team members should understand and be able to communicate which of those kinds of authority is vested with the team. Defining the type of authority the team will have may require negotiations with your boss, the team's sponsor, and key stakeholders. A shared understanding of team authority among this group is essential during team formation.

When the Buck Doesn't Stop, the Team Does

A cross-functional team is formed to accelerate new product development. After each meeting the team members return to their department heads and report what the team has decided. But each time, the department heads have objections to the team's decision and withhold support. Subsequently, team members return to the team and ask for another round of decision making. Because people outside of the team have veto power over the team's decisions, the team is unable to meet its goal.

Reward team performance. Organizations tend to reward individual performance. But rewards that focus on individual achievements rather than group achievements won't help to motivate your team and won't make team members feel valued and supported for the work they do in support of the team's goals. Without a team-oriented reward system, people may refuse to serve on teams or resent being appointed to teams.

As you set up your team, establish rewards for team performance. Money is one such reward (for example, linking an individual's bonus to team results), but financial compensation should be only one part of your team reward system. Other reward tactics to consider include:

- *Recognition.* Signal that team success really counts in your company with articles in the company newsletter, team retreats, t-shirts and other paraphernalia.
- *Education.* Promote the learning aspects of being on a team. Acquiring new skills and knowledge is always part of the team experience, and that gives team members more options for their future and more control over their careers.
- *Travel.* Many team assignments provide opportunities for getting out of the office. If team members come from several locations, an attractive destination for meetings can be a reward.

- *Promotion.* Explain that people commonly emerge from a team assignment ready to take on new challenges and handle new responsibilities – making them more valuable to the organization and in the marketplace.

- *Celebration.* Because successful teams often accomplish a one-time goal, reward that unique contribution with a social event, a group photograph, a chance to tell stories of teamwork, and an opportunity to record successes and lessons learned. A team that accomplishes its goal is likely to experience some euphoria when it reaches the end, and a celebration provides an outlet for emotional release, for reflection, for recognition, and for extending that energy into the rest of the organization.

Create an Empowering Team Structure

Building a team involves creating a structure that helps it maximize its resources. Creating that enabling structure is one of the most challenging aspects of team formation. It involves determining team functions, defining team member roles and responsibilities, defining what competencies will be needed for the team to do its work and accomplish its goal, setting the size of the team, determining how team leadership will be handled, and managing team stability.

Identify team functions. Team functional areas are the sets of capabilities that the team needs not only to do its work but to be able to work effectively as a team. Important functional areas include:

- *Task/technical.* Specific skills directly related to accomplishing the team's goal(s) are required.

- *Key relationships.* Specific skills in advancing the team's goal(s) by effectively informing, negotiating, and influencing stakeholders and other individuals and organizations with whom the team interfaces are part of this critical communications function.

- *Monitoring.* Your team will need to gather and analyze information from sources external to the team that is relevant to the team's goal(s).
- *Maintenance.* Your team will want to enhance its own internal relationships and cooperation through openness, conflict management, interpersonal skills, humor, and tact.
- *Authority.* A critical team function involves inspiring team members and directing the team toward accomplishing its goal(s) by maintaining focus, clarifying expectations, strategizing, organizing, and aligning work with the team's goal(s).

A common mistake managers make when forming a team is to not move beyond the task / technical function that is most directly related to the team's goal. While this function is obviously important for the team's success, the other four team-level functions reflect the need to manage the processes, relationships, and changes that occur inside and outside of the team. These functional areas are equally vital to assembling an effective team.

Determine team roles. Once you have identified team functional areas you will need to determine the specific roles and / or responsibilities needed to represent those functions. When defining roles for functional areas you may need team members with specific jobs to support the task / technical functions. For example, the team may require a salesperson with a strong background in telecommunication.

Beyond technical roles, you will also need to determine the specific roles or responsibilities that represent the other four functional areas. It's important to recognize that specific team roles, which support specific functional areas, can shift from one team member to another. Additionally, team functions may be represented by more than one role. When forming your team, consider the entire spectrum of what the team requires for success, then define the appropriate functions that match those requirements and

Team Resources Worksheet

Resources	Need? Yes/No	Description	Cost	Date Requested	Approval	Notes
1. Physical space a) Individual b) Work area c) Meetings						
2. Equipment a) b)						
3. Software/systems a) b) c)						

Team Resources Worksheet (continued)

Resources	Need? Yes/No	Description	Cost	Date Requested	Approval	Notes
4. Education/ training a) Individual b) Team building						
5. Rewards a) Individual b) Team recognition						
6. External staff a) Support b) Consultants/ experts						
7. Budget a) Operating b) Capital						

the specific roles that represent those functions.

Define team member competencies. Competencies are knowledge, skills, and experience individuals possess that enable them to be successful in a given role or situation. Forming an effective team involves your determining the skills, knowledge, and experience that are needed to fill the team roles you have identified as crucial to your team's success. Those competencies include technical skills, content knowledge, and interpersonal skills.

Technical competency. Technical competencies include expertise and skills in developing and using the business processes and systems that affect the team's work. For example, most teams need members who can determine what information the team needs and how it will gather, store, and use that information. Other technical requirements may demand specific expertise and experience. Your team may, for

Team Leader Role

The role of team leader is a key role that needs to be clearly defined early on in the team formation process. Not all teams have leaders, but all teams have leadership responsibilities, such as convening the team, assigning work, monitoring individual and team performance, moderating discussions, and facilitating decision making. In planning how your team will handle these leadership responsibilities, consider these questions:

- Will the team have a designated leader or will it be a leaderless team?
- Will team leadership rotate?
- Will leadership responsibilities be shared among the team members? If so, how will that sharing be worked out?
- What decisions will the leader make without involving team members?
- What decisions will the leader make with the input of team members?
- What decisions will the leader delegate to the team members?

example, need someone who is very familiar with the customer-service system or someone who participated in the restructuring of your organization's manufacturing processes.

Content competency. A team that lacks crucial facts or doesn't understand organizational history will find it difficult to get results that are accurate and ultimately accepted by others outside the team. A search committee needs to know current compensation rates, for example. Teams may have to go beyond their membership to get some of the information they need, but the critical core of knowledge should be held and understood by team members.

Interpersonal competency. In addition to technical knowledge and content expertise, people also bring to the team their thinking styles, communication skills, and skills (or lack thereof) at handling interpersonal relationships. You will likely need team members who are good at communication, negotiation, and persuasion. Interpersonal competencies are particularly important for roles and responsibilities linked to the team's key relationships, maintenance, and leadership functions that are essential for a team's success.

Fit competencies to roles. Not all people can have all the necessary competencies your team needs or even all the skills needed for any given team role. Team members inevitably have different experiences and talents. Those differences are important during team formation. Diversity among team members provides balance and can help teams perform more effectively by allowing individual perspectives, various backgrounds, and certain capabilities to be applied to the team's work. This kind of diversity is particularly important when the work of a team is complex.

With the idea of diversified backgrounds, perspectives, and capabilities in mind, your goal at this stage is to evaluate team candidates to determine what skills, knowledge, and abilities they can bring to bear on the team's roles and tasks, and to select team members accordingly. You can use the Team Candidate Interview Worksheet on page 21 to help you formulate questions specific to the needs of the team you are forming.

There are formal and informal methods to evaluate team candidates and to identify their competencies. Formal methods include getting input from your company's human resources department, from the candidate's current and/or past bosses, and from employee performance reviews. These resources can provide insight into the personal characteristics

Most Teams Need . . .

- analytical skills
- listening skills
- strategic thinking ability
- logistic ability
- conflict resolution skills
- attention to detail
- skills in problem identification and problem solving
- creativity
- facilitating and summarizing abilities
- organizational savvy

and work ethics that potential team members possess. There are also informal methods that you can use to evaluate the skills, knowledge, and abilities of team candidates. These methods include studying what potential team members have produced and how, conversing with current and potential team members about key job experiences and past team experiences, and connecting with colleagues outside of the team who have experience with current and potential team members to learn about the roles and responsibilities that team members took on in the past.

Decide on team size. The number of team members you select depends on the competencies and roles required for your team to be successful. You may have to include people from several departments in order to give your team the broad range of knowledge and skills it needs. The more complex the problem or goal(s), the more roles and competencies your team is likely to need. Six members may be too few if the assignment is complex and if all six members are still responsible for their regular jobs or if the team needs to be subdivided to accomplish certain tasks. Twelve team members may be too many because individuals might feel less

Team Candidate Interview Worksheet

Use the examples in this worksheet to help you create specific questions relevant to your team's situation and task. After conducting your interviews you will be in a good position to match candidate attributes to the team roles you previously defined. This information means you are more likely to make good team member selections, which is crucial to effective team formation.

Competencies	Questions
Skills	What technical proficiency do you possess related to the team's goals?
	What task-related experience have you had related to the team's goals?
	What examples of work product do you have related to the team's goals?
Knowledge	What training have you had that's related to the team's goals?
	What educational degrees do you have related to the team's goals?
	What informal training have you had related to the team's goals?
Experience	Describe a time when you worked in a team in which authority was not clear. What did you do to establish and maintain effective working relationships with the team leader and other team members?
	Describe a situation in which you were faced with a team conflict. How did you deal with it?
	Describe a time when you had to persuade others of your idea, point of view, or solution. How did you proceed? What have you done when team members wouldn't go along with you?
	Describe the most difficult person with whom you have had to deal in a team. How did you handle that situation?
	Describe a situation in which you developed goals with your workgroup or team. What was the process you followed?
	Describe a time when you played a key role in helping your team obtain its goals and objectives. How did you contribute?

responsible and accountable for team results, and because communications, meeting schedules, and other logistical considerations become more difficult to manage.

Consider team stability. One way to ensure a team's focus and its ability to stay on schedule is to select members who will be available for the life of the team. When team members drop out you have to replace them, and the team's performance will drop as it assimilates new members.

Distance can also influence a team's stability. If some team members are out of the country, for example, or otherwise unable to attend meetings, the team will have to postpone meetings or it will have to hold meetings and carry on its work without all of the information, perspectives, and skills that are usually at its disposal.

Identify Key Relationships

No team operates in a vacuum. As you form your team, keep in mind that in addition to selecting the right team members and building internal processes, you will need to identify important stakeholders in and outside of the organization. The stakeholders can include team sponsors, customers, business partners, and competitors. The degree to which you need to develop these relationships depends upon your team's tasks, but at the least your team will require some understanding of the necessity of building and maintaining solid relationships with critical others outside the team.

You can start developing key relationships by paying special attention to how you introduce the team to the organization and how you explain the criteria used to select team members. Before your team meets for the first time, announce its formation to the organization. (In this case *organization* can be a department or division of a company, or it may be the entire company.) Consider using all the usual channels of communication: all-hands meetings, employee newsletters, e-mail, and bulletin boards, for example. Your announcement should clearly state your team's purpose, the organization's expectations for your team's work, the names of team members, and the timeframe – if applicable – established for the team's work.

The following questions will help you identify stakeholders and determine the intensity of key relationships your team will require to perform at a high level.

- How will your team's goals extend into the boundaries of other teams or workgroups? What relationships will it need among business units, sales and marketing groups, customers, and perhaps even your competitors?
- What information and/or resources will your team require from other individuals or teams to complete its work?
- What relationships will your team need to have with individuals or teams in other organizations to complete its work?
- How will your team function effectively within the broader context of the organization and its visions, values, and practices?
- Who are the stakeholders critical to your team's success?
- If expectations change as your team proceeds with its work, who needs to be aware of these changes?
- Will your team interact with external clients? Are their needs well defined and consistent, or are they subject to change? Are external client contact relationships stable, or do contacts change periodically?
- Will external stakeholders evaluate your team's work? What is the nature of the evaluation? Is regular feedback from external stakeholders crucial to your team's success? If yes, how will your team receive this feedback?
- How will your team respond to feedback from outsiders? Will you have a mechanism in place for responding to feedback? Will outsiders know when their feedback has been incorporated into team processes or products?

- How will communication and coordination between your team and other relevant individuals/groups be managed?
- What publicity and communication channels are available to your team?
- How will your team's purposes, capabilities, and performance be communicated on a regular basis?

Monitor External Factors

The team you form will operate not just in an environment conditioned by the requirements and culture of your organization, but will also be subject to environmental factors inside and outside the organization. Identifying and maintaining an awareness of environmental influences, demands, and changes can help you build a team that can reach a higher level of performance.

By considering external factors during team formation, you can design a team that doesn't just react to change but maintains an awareness of change. The following questions will help you form a team that not only stays informed of external factors that may affect its performance but forms strategies to deal with those factors and learns how to capitalize on change.

- What economic pressures/trends will impact team formation/development in the next five years?
- To what degree will your team be directly affected by market changes?
- What continuing technological advances will change team work or team composition in the next five years?
- To what degree will your team be affected by changing technologies?
- What demographic changes will continue to impact team design and composition?

- Will your organization need to establish a basic skills program in order to have a pool of potential team members with the level of knowledge that team members in general need to have?

- Who are your top five competitors? What are they doing? Do they present opportunities or potential problems?

- What persons or teams outside your team's boundaries is your team dependent upon for information, support, or other needs, and to what degree?

- Does globalization affect your team's purpose or its processes? For example, how might you manage a team that deals with local rules and regulations other than those of the country in which you are headquartered?

If your responses to these questions indicate to you that you need to better understand the impact of external factors on your team(s), then you will need to gather information and learn about strategies for successfully handling external factors. One tactic might be to visit other organizations to see how other teams operate, broadening your perspective and providing new ideas for how you can form a team with an awareness of external factors. The External Factors Checklist on page 26 can help guide your thinking about how your team's overall goals and strategy will be affected by the external environment and how your team will deal with those influences.

External Factors Checklist

❏ My team has a plan for identifying, gathering, analyzing, and disseminating relevant information.

❏ Team members will use skills such as active listening, asking questions, exchanging relevant information, and dialoguing in interacting with outsiders.

❏ Team members will act as "generalists" in their approach to information gathering.

❏ Training in information-gathering skills is available to team members as needed.

❏ Team members will probe internal sources to exchange information with other members who represent outside stakeholder interests.

❏ New information will impact team decisions.

❏ My team will test what it learns in the field.

❏ Lessons from field tests and external evaluations will be incorporated into how my team does its work.

❏ My team-selection criteria includes the ability to be comfortable with changes in the team's goals and intended results in response to outside information.

Team Formation: A Special Event

Forming a team doesn't take care of itself. To form a team that has real potential for success, you should pay careful attention to the five principles discussed in this guidebook. Give your team a clear direction, investigate organizational support, build a team structure that is supportive of the team's goals and the team's members, map the key relationships your team will need to build inside and outside of the organization, and be sure to have a plan for monitoring external factors.

Team formation is a special event. Team results are dependent on a good team design, one that accounts for team support, team communication, and team rewards. When a team is formed with those principles in mind, it has a good chance of reaching success.

Suggested Readings

Dyer, W. G. (1995). *Team building, current issues and new alternatives* (3rd ed.). Reading, MA: Addison-Wesley.

Hallam, G. L. (1996). *The adventures of Team Fantastic.* Greensboro, NC: Center for Creative Leadership.

Hughes, R. L., Ginnett, R. C., & Curphy, G. J. (1996). *Leadership: Enhancing the lessons of experience* (2nd ed.). Boston, MA: Irwin McGraw-Hill.

Isgar, T. (1989). *The ten-minute team: 10 steps to building high performing teams.* Boulder, CO: Selura Press.

Katzenbach, J. R. (1998). *Teams at the top: Unleashing the potential of both teams and individual leaders.* Boston, MA: Harvard Business School Press.

Katzenbach, J. R., & Smith, D. K. (1993). *The wisdom of teams.* Boston, MA: Harvard Business School Press.

Kossler, M. E., & Kanaga, K. (2001). *Do you really need a team?* Greensboro, NC: Center for Creative Leadership.

Lipnack, J., & Stamps, J. (1993). *The TeamNet Factor: Bringing the power of boundary crossing into the heart of your business.* New York: Wiley.

McVinney, C. (1999). Dream weaver. *Training & Development, 53*(4), 38-42.

Nadler, D. A. (1998). Executive team effectiveness: Teamwork at the top. In D. A. Nadler, J. L. Spencer, & Associates (Eds.), *Executive teams* (pp. 21-39). San Francisco: Jossey-Bass.

Reddy, W. B., & Jamison, K. (Eds.). (1988). *Team building: Blueprints for productivity and satisfaction.* Alexandria, VA: NTL Institute for Applied Behavioral Science.

Scholtes, P. R., Joiner, B. L., & Streibel, B. J. (1996). *The team handbook* (2nd rev. ed.). Madison, WI: Oriel Inc.

Sessa, V. I., Hansen, M. C., Prestridge, S., & Kossler, M. E. (1999). *Geographically dispersed teams: An annotated bibliography.* Greensboro, NC: Center for Creative Leadership.

Yeats, D. E., & Hyten, C. (1998). *High performing self-managed work teams.* Thousand Oaks, CA: Sage Publications.

Background

Since the mid-1980s, the Center for Creative Leadership (CCL) has worked with many organizations and teams through its educational initiatives. The goal of these initiatives is to help participants develop team management skills through a proven process that combines personal assessment, feedback from the workplace, and experience with practical team-oriented applications. These developmental experiences provide research-based information about how high-performance teams work, honest appraisals of existing teams' strengths and weaknesses, and proven approaches for turning average performers into a highly effective team. It covers such issues as selecting team members, launching teams effectively, bridging cross-cultural differences in teams, and resolving team conflict. Through training programs, research, and custom interventions, CCL continues to provide a hands-on learning experience for team leaders that emphasizes a range of practical tools and strategies for enhancing the performance of any team.

In addition to providing these team-oriented educational programs and customized interventions, CCL launched in 1996 a research project into the work and performance of geographically dispersed teams. Since 1997, various CCL faculty members have presented their findings and analyses at conferences and through various publications. CCL continues its work with clients and with other scholars to further develop its understanding of teams – how they can be led more effectively, how they can best achieve organizational goals, and how they can be created and maintained for improved results. CCL seeks to pass that understanding on to team leaders and their organizations in order that teams meet and even surpass performance expectations.

Key Point Summary

One of the first steps to take toward increasing team effectiveness is to pay attention to how the team is formed. You can head off most of the problems that beset teams during the formation stage by setting a clear direction, securing organizational support, building an enabling team structure, developing key relationships, and monitoring external factors.

For members of a team to work effectively together, they need to have a shared understanding of why the team exists and what the team members are expected to accomplish. Team members should be able to state the team's purpose in a simple, direct way and be able to communicate that purpose to all stakeholders in a consistent manner.

Make special efforts to ensure that your organization supports the team you're forming with adequate resources, organizational sponsorship, recognition of team member responsibility and team authority, a means of providing feedback on performance, and a team-oriented reward system.

> **The 5 Keys to Forming an Effective Team**
>
> 1. Set a clear direction.
> 2. Build organizational support.
> 3. Create an empowering team structure.
> 4. Identify key relationships.
> 5. Monitor external factors.

The actual structure of the team also helps it to be successful. Designing a strong team defines, among other things, team member responsibilities (which team members will play what roles on the team) and determines what technical and interpersonal skills the team needs to accomplish its task.

In addition to selecting the right team members and building internal processes, you will need to identify important stakeholders in and outside of the organization. The degree to which you need to develop these relationships depends upon your team's tasks, but at the least your team should have some understanding of the necessity of building and maintaining solid relationships outside the team.

The team you form will be subject to environmental factors inside and outside the organization. Identifying and maintaining an awareness of environmental influences, demands, and changes can help you build a team that can achieve a higher level of performance. The team you form won't just react to change but maintains an awareness of change.

Organizations seek high performance from their teams. When you form a team using the five principles described in this guidebook, it has a good chance of meeting those expectations.

ORDER FORM

To order, complete and return a copy of this form or contact the Center's Publication Area at: Post Office Box 26300 • Greensboro, NC 27438-6300 • Phone 336-545-2810 • Fax 336-282-3284. You can also order via the Center's online bookstore at www.ccl.org/publications

	QUANTITY	SUBTOTAL
❑ I would like to order additional copies of **How to Form a Team: Five Keys to High Performance** (#414) $8.95 ea.*		
❑ I would like to order other Ideas Into Action Guidebooks.		
❑ **Ongoing Feedback** (#400) $8.95 ea.*		
❑ **Reaching Your Development Goals** (#401) $8.95 ea.*		
❑ **Becoming a More Versatile Learner** (#402) $8.95 ea.*		
❑ **Giving Feedback to Subordinates** (#403) $8.95 ea.*		
❑ **Three Keys to Development** (#404) $8.95 ea.*		
❑ **Feedback That Works** (#405) $8.95 ea.*		
❑ **Communicating Across Cultures** (#406) $8.95 ea.*		
❑ **Learning from Life** (#407) $8.95 ea.*		
❑ **Keeping Your Career on Track** (#408) $8.95 ea.*		
❑ **Preparing for Development** (#409) $8.95 ea.*		
❑ **Choosing an Executive Coach** (#410) $8.95 ea.*		
❑ **Setting Your Development Goals** (#411) $8.95 ea.*		
❑ **Do You Really Need a Team?** (#412) $8.95 ea.*		
❑ **Building Resiliency** (#413) $8.95 ea.*		
❑ **Feedback Package** (#724; includes #400, #403, #405) $17.95 ea.		
❑ **Individual Leadership Development Package** (#726; includes #401, #404, #409, #411) $26.95 ea.		
Add sales tax if resident of CA (7.5%), CO (6%), NC (6.5%)	SALES TAX	
U.S. shipping (UPS Ground – $4 for 1st book; $0.95 each additional book) Non-U.S. shipping (Express International – $20 for 1st book; $5 each additional book)	SHIPPING	
CCL's Federal Tax ID #23-707-9591	TOTAL	

*Single title quantity discounts: 5-99 – $7.95; 100-499 – $6.50; 500+ – $5.95

DISCOUNTS ARE AVAILABLE
IF ORDERING BY MAIL OR FAX, PLEASE COMPLETE INFORMATION BELOW.

PAYMENT

❏ My check or money order is enclosed. **(Prepayment required for orders less than \$100.)**

❏ Charge my order, plus shipping, to my credit card.
  ❏ American Express   ❏ Discover   ❏ MasterCard   ❏ Visa

  Acct. # _____   Expiration Date: Mo. / Yr. _____

  Name as appears on card _____

  Signature of card holder _____

SHIP TO

Name _____

Title _____

Organization _____

Street Address _____

City / State / Zip _____

Phone (_____) _____
Your telephone number is required for shipping.

❏ CHECK HERE TO RECEIVE A COMPLETE GUIDE TO CCL PUBLICATIONS.
❏ CHECK HERE TO RECEIVE INFORMATION ABOUT CCL PROGRAMS AND PRODUCTS.

ORDER BY PHONE: 336-545-2810 • ONLINE: WWW.CCL.ORG/PUBLICATIONS